D1581442

REDS GREATEST
SPACE CADET

30118134125719

Bloomsbury Education
An imprint of Bloomsbury Publishing Plc

50 Bedford Square
London
WC1B 3DP
UK

1385 Broadway
New York
NY 10018
USA

www.bloomsbury.com

BLOOMSBURY and the Diana logo are trademarks of Bloomsbury Publishing Plc

First published in 2017 by Bloomsbury Education

To find out more about our authors and books visit www.bloomsbury.com.
Here you will find extracts, author interviews, details of forthcoming events
and the option to sign up for our newsletters.

POEMS BY JAMES CARTER

Illustrated by ED BOXALL

THE WORLD'S GREATEST SPACE CADET

BLOOMSBURY EDUCATION
AN IMPRINT OF BLOOMSBURY
LONDON OXFORD NEW YORK NEW DELHI SYDNEY

For Stephen Blackburn – one of the finest,
kindest humans on the planet

'School Library' is for the marvellous Mrs P and everyone
at the rather wonderful Falkland Primary School in Newbury,

'Five Ways To Cross The River' is for Down-Under-David,

'So You Want To Build A Bear...' is for Yukon John,

'Baby Ukulele' is for Chris and Daisy,

'What Is It?' is for Ardingly College
(and their uber-librarian Denise Reed),

'A Hill' is for Sarah, Lauren and Madeleine.

And more than thanks to Ed Boxall
for bringing so much of his magic to this book.

CONTENTS

AHA!

Aha! Hurrah! Hip-
hip hooray! I had this
great idea today. Boof! It
came, as ideas do — as if a gift
from out the blue. What was
it now, you want to know?
Oh, botherations, drat and
blow. How absolutely
jolly rotten. See,
I've utterly
forgotten
!!!!!!!!!!!!!
!!!!!!!!!!
!! !!

★ 1 ★

FOR MY FRIEND

WHO'S
THE HOT DOG
THE COOL BEANS
THE BEE'S KNEES
THE BIG CHEESE
THE TOP BANANA
CAT'S PYJAMAS
CHERRY COLA
SUPERNOVA
EVER-STELLAR
MEGASTAR
BESTEST BOD
ON EARTH
BY FAR?

DON'T YOU KNOW?

YOU ARE!

SPACE CADET

A *dreamer?*
Me? Err, you bet, the
world's greatest space cadet!
I'm **alien** in **human** form. Some
distant **planet** I was born. Although
these feet are on the **ground**, my head
is firmly in a **cloud**. A **dolly daydream**
you might say, my **mind** is always miles
away, cruisin' 'round the **Milky Way** —
or maybe further, sure is far, for all
I hear is **blah blah blah**.
Me? I've been like this
since **birth**...

ARE YOU LISTENING

PLANET
EARTH?!?

★ 4 ★

THE MOUSE THAT FELL TO EARTH

(HAIKU)

A grey mouse, still warm,
but limp and newly lifeless,
lies on the back lawn.

A red kite swoops, squeals,
screeches angrily above,
having dropped its meal.

A black cat arrives,
grabs the gift between its teeth;
leaves, eats in private.

SID

You've never met a cat
quite like Sid. He's a brute.
He's a bruiser. He's a bully, he is,
that cat from two doors down.

Sid Vicious I call him.
You should see the way
he terrifies and torments
our kittens. He's fearless.
He'd take the kill from an eagle,
the carrion from a crow.
If he was human, he'd be
forever behind bars.

When he walks, he doesn't slink
as much as plod and stomp.
He breathes heavy.
He snarls. He scowls.

And don't you be fooled by
those delicate whiskers, those
pretty white mittens. Check out
those eyes. Deeper
than an old well. Greener
than a witch's brew.

And that coat, blacker
than the night when
the stars were stolen.

He'd pick on anyone, Sid,
anything, any size.

However tough your cat is,
don't let it out tonight.

Sid wins *every* fight.

IF I PROMISE...

...to feed it,
to care for
and clean it,
to love it, to hug it,
to pat it, to pet it,
to never forget it,
oh big mega-pleasy,
oh sweet lemon-squeezy –
please could we *please*
get a pet... cat?

NO!

Dog?

NO!

Poisonous yellow frog?

NO!

Tank of iguanas?
School of piranhas?
Blue-bottomed monkeys,
all snuffling bananas?

Ohhhhhhhhhhhhhhh...*

(* = you always know the answer's 'no',
but keep on asking, hassling daily –
eventually, you'll drive 'em C R A Z Y...)

THE MONKEY AND THE APPLE

Whipsnade Zoo, summer 2012

Monkey doesn't seem to notice
the rain or even the noisy tourists
for his mind is on the apple

left over from feeding time,
the red one that bobs half-afloat
on the surface of the little lake.

After several moments of head-slapping
and chin-scratching, Monkey disappears,
returning with the twiggiest of sticks

to prod the apple, over and again,
attempting to bring it back to shore.
Admitting defeat, he chucks his tool

onto the water and it's only then
that he greets his audience, graces
them with a 'whatever' gaze, an almost

'you get it, if you're that smart' sneer,
before scrambling off into the late
afternoon of the trees.

RAT-A-TUT-TUT!

You humans are
such silly creatures.
Just a load
of picky eaters.

'Mummy, dear!'
I hear you shout.
'Please don't make
eat a sprout!'

And, 'Tell me,
is this broccoli?
Are you to trying
to *poison* me?'

Humans – waste
your food and cash.
Rats aren't fussed.
We'll eat your trash!

HOW MANY MINIBEASTS?

A *stampede* of millipedes?
A *festival* of fleas?
An *earful* of earwigs?
A *business* of bees?

A *scuttling* of ladybugs?
A *squadron* of wasps?
A *rock 'n roll* of dung beetles?
A *discotheque* of moths?

A *fidgeting* of earthworms?
A *nastiness* of nits?
A *beastliness* of minibeasts?
This poem makes me *itch*!

SPIDER, SPIDER . . .

... hear my rhyme!
Do you think you'll spare
the time to spin a little web tonight? From sticky silk in cold moon-
light? You weave away. You scuttle free.
Your artistry's an alchemy, of science, maths
and harmony. A masterpiece of symmetry. A
clever, clinging web design. A classic, Gothic
house divine. Your magic number? No surprise. You have eight legs. You have eight
eyes. Little dancer, have you heard?
Your web's 8th Wonder
of the World...

CONVERSATION WITH A FLY

ZZZZ!

Oh, hello, fly!

ZZZZ!

What are you up to, then?

ZZZZ!

Sorry, I didn't catch that...

ZZZZ!

No, I still didn't get it.

ZZZZ!

Are you trying to tell me something?

ZZZZ!

Something important, perhaps?

ZZZZ!

Is something the matter, maybe?

ZZZZ!

Are you in some kind of trouble?

ZZZZ!

Look. I don't understand 'zzzz!'

ZZZZ!

Please don't keep saying 'zzzz!'

ZZZZ!

Right, fly. I'll give you one more chance – **OKAY**?

ZZZZZ!!!!!

BEASTLY ME

I'm the *wasp* that will not sting.
The *bear* that leaves the honey.
The happy *bird* that will not sing.
The *sloth* that's in a hurry.

The *tiger shark* that has no teeth.
The *spider* cute, not hairy.
The *centipede* that has two feet.
I'm *beastly* and *contrary*...

ELEPHANT

Where on earth
would you begin
to paint an elephant?

That quick-witted,
ocean-memoried,
grey hunk of a thing?

Linking
tail-to-trunk
to-tail-to-trunk,
over the
dusty plains?

Marching through
the clatter
of some summer
street parade?

Or alone
out there
in the starry dark,
turning over
the cold bones
of one long gone?

And what would
you paint it with?

Colours
or words?

SCHOOL LIBRARY!

Where are doorways made of words?
That open onto other worlds?
Welcoming all boys and girls?

SCHOOL LIBRARY!

Enter stories wild as dreams.
Meet aliens or fairy queens.
If fun-filled facts are more your scene…

SCHOOL LIBRARY!

Listen, they've got everything,
to make you chuckle, giggle, grin –
be spooked or thrilled. Just come on in.

SCHOOL LIBRARY!

Tempted? Go on, have a look.
You never know, you might get hooked.
Your whole life changed by just one book…

SCHOOL LIBRARY!

HOW TO TURN YOUR TEACHER PURPLE!

Heebie Geebie, Hurple Burple –
Time To Turn My Teacher
PURPLE!

Simply chant this magic spell.
Soon your teacher looks unwell.
Purple cheeks and purple nose.
Purpleness from head to toes.

Feed her beetroot every hour.
See her fill with purple power.
Bloomin' like a purple flower.
How she'll screeeeeeeeeeam
when in the shower!!!

Heebie Geebie, Hurple Burple –
Time To Turn My Teacher...

★ 22 ★

HOW TO BE YOUR TEACHER'S FAVOURITE

Try reading this aloud in class...

You're a *TURBO-TEACHER*, yes you are.
A *SUPER-POWERED* megastar!

Your *X-RAY EYES* don't miss a thing.
Your *ROBOT-BRAIN* knows *e v e r y t h i n g .*

Your *FAIRIES' FEET* can zip around.
Your *CAT-LIKE EARS* hear every sound.

Your *DOG-LIKE SNOUT* can sniff us out.
But can you *MIND-READ*? We've no doubt...

Yet you've an *ANGEL'S HEART*, oh yes.
As with great kindness we are blessed.

Now why d'you think I'm saying this?
As people diss you teachers, Miss.

But you're a *HIT*, a *WHIZZ*, a *WOW*...
can I be your favourite now?

★ 23 ★

WHAT TO SAY IF YOU MEET A GHOST...

```
                Aaa
              aaaaaaa
              aaaaaaa
!!!           aaaaaa           !!!
 !!           aaaaa             !!
  !!           aaa             !!
   !!      aaaaaaa      !!
      aaaaaaaaaaaaaa
    aaaaaaaaaaaaaaaaa
   aaaaaaaaaaaaaaaaaaa
  aaaaaaaaaaaaaaaaaaaaa
   aaaaaaaaaaaaaaaaaaa
    aaaaaaaaaaaaaaaa
     aaaaaaaaaaaaaa
      aaaaaaaaaa
      aaaaaaa
         hhhh
          hhh
          hhh
          hh
          hh
          h
          !
          !
```

GRANDAD, AFTER THE WAR

I never met my Grandad, my Mum's Dad. He died before I was born. And no-one ever said much about him, except when I asked. They didn't seem to miss him much. They said he went off to war, the Great War, to fight in the trenches. Came back a different man, they said: quiet, distant, detached.

On the day of his final return, they all gazed out the windows at him. He'd worn that uniform for weeks and weeks and it was now stuck to his lanky, skeletal frame, for it was thick with grime and earth and god knows what else, they said. Grandma wouldn't let him into the house until he'd removed it all in the street. Fine welcome home for a soldier.

No, Grandad didn't talk much after the war, they said, about the war or anything. He'd get back from his job at the butcher's shop and sit and doze in his chair, they said. So who knows what fears, what horrors still burnt behind his sleeping eyes, what muddy ghosts still visited him all those years after, for he never mentioned a word of it.

WHAT TO SAY WHEN OLAF 'OLAF' OLAFSSON (A VERY HUNGRY, ANCIENT VIKING WARRIOR) TURNS UP TOTALLY UNEXPECTEDLY FOR SUPPER ONE SATURDAY EVENING...

Olaf, please don't
think I'm rude.
But that's our cat,
and he's not food.

Put Mittens down.
And my brother.
Seriously. They're not
your supper.

Put the door back.
Now relax.
We'll sort you out
some tasty snacks.

Weirdy Beardy –
come and see...
The Axe Factor
is on TV!

US?

```
     υυυυυυυυυυυ
   υυυυυυυυυυυυυυυ
 υυυυυυυυυυυυυυυυυυ
 @         υυυυ          @
 @   +++   υυυυ   +++   @
 @    V    υυυυ    V    @
 @         υυυυ          @
 @          V           @
   @                  @
   @    We were...   @
     @              @
       @ @ @
```

Dark Agers,
land invaders, craft
traders, ocean gravers, myth-
!! makers, longboat sailors, wave !!
!! riders, fierce fighters, strong !!
!! survivors, kenning scribers, !!
!! Nordic dwellers, beardy !!
!! fellas. At thieving bling !!
 !! we were the best, we !!
 !!! were The Vikings !!!
... had you
guessed?
```
       ???
      ??  ??
      ??  ??
      ??  ??
      ??  ??
     ????   ????
```

★ 28 ★

GHOST SHIPS

To solve the secrets of the past
maybe we should ask the stars:
for they're the watchers of the skies
with their ever gazey eyes

To them my question would be this:
what happened to the pirate ships?
Are they somewhere, way out there,
where sea meets sky, and water, air?

Pirates left their lives of crime
but do their ships still drift through time?
And do the timbers creak and groan
as they heave through storms alone?

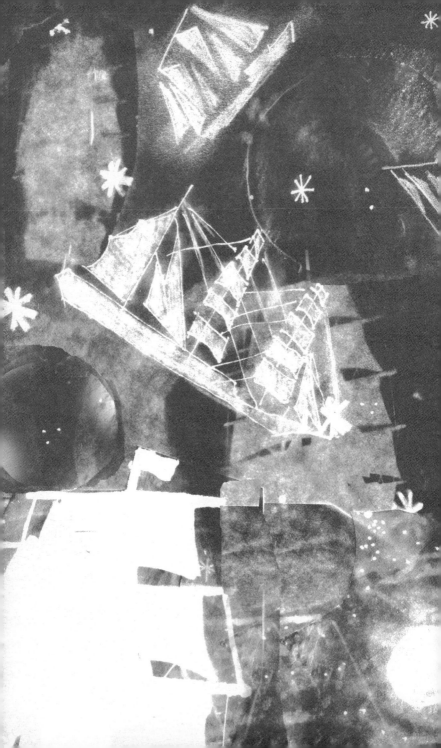

And have their sails, their flags of bones,
been cut to shreds and tempest-blown?
Come stars, reveal – please do tell all:
do these ghost ships tumble, fall

off the edge of ocean green
through the sky to space serene
and whilst they glide through endless night –
stars, d'you guide them with your light?

NOW...

The birth of a star.
The beat of a heart.

The arc of an hour.
The bee and the flower.

The flight of a swan.
The weight of the sun.

A river in flood.
The nature of blood.

The future in space
for this human race.

Now that's
what I call
science

WHAT WOULD YOU ASK AN ASTRONAUT?

Science Museum, autumn half-term

A silver-haired American man stands beside a space craft
he tells us is a Lunar Module. He wears an off-white
spacesuit, and in nearly whispered tones he brings his time
in space to life there in that room.

We don't ask him anything, as he tells it all, as well as how,
even now, his dreams are mostly of the moon. And as he
talks we see that mighty *Saturn Five* rocket surging up and
through the clouds, and him floating weightless, listening
to those crackled voices calling from the earth. We too feel
that gentle thud when landing on the lunar soil.

We watch him taking leaps across that old, grey world,
leaving all those footprints that remain there in the sand.
Most of all, we marvel as he spots a perfect opal, blue and
swirly white, high in the moon's sky, and realises it's home.

And does it matter he's an actor? Or the module just a
model? Not a bit, for still we walk away all starry-eyed.

WHAT I WANT

I want to be invisible

sky
the
touch
to
want
I

I
want
to catch a
st★r to-
night

                                          y
                                     l
I want two wings to   *f*

★ 34 ★

I want to travel   far in time

and
space
to places
N E W

IWANTTOWALKTHROUGHTHICKBRICKWALLS

I

want it

A L L

Don't you?

WHAT IS THE WORLD?

A scientist may say:
'70% water, 30% land.'

A geologist may say:
'4 1/2 billion years old.'

An astronomer may say:
'The
merest speck
on a cosmic coast
awash on the tide of time.'

A myth-maker may say:
'A glorious orb
held aloft
by
elephants
atop a giant turtle.'

A priest may say:
'A miracle.'

An astronaut may say:
'Home.'

An ecologist may say:
'Poorly.'

THE LIGHT

We live
for the light.

Like flowers,
our heads
ever turn
where it's bright.

We yearn when dark
for the planet to spin,
for the light to return
and for life to begin.

Without it,
we wither.
We sleepwalk
through winter.

Moon, tell the sun
to spark out the night.
We need to be loved,
be touched by the light.

SEASONS 4

AUTUMN'S a breeze
that sneaks 'round trees
and tickles them 'til
they lose their leaves

WINTER'S a gust
of huffs and puffs –
the gifts it gives are
sniffs and coughs

SPRING'S a tweet
a pulse a beat
a dance to lift our
hearts and feet

SUMMER'S a hoot
and hot that's what
a chance to do
well not a lot!

WHAT IS IT?

I'll tell you what it is.
The gymnasiu**M** of your brain.
A way to escape, without going out.

The home of **G**reat ideas.
A portal to all poss**I**bilities.
A road to the unknow**N**.

Fant**A**sy. Fiction. Fun. Free.
A quiet place to **T**hink things through.
A world that asks 'W*hat* **I***f*...?'

Somewhere **O**nly you can see
(though every huma**N** has one).
Use yours to work it out...**!**

HEY, POEM!

Tell me something
I don't know –

like how do clouds
make all that snow?

Or dazzle me,
or make me think,

weave wonders there
in that black ink,

or give me secrets,
riddles, lies,

a little thought,
a big surprise –

poem, work your
magic, do –

but most of all
say something NEW...

BABY UKULELE!

The
guitar
has had
a baby.
It's
call
-ed
the
uku
-lele.
A funny
little strummy
thing. You can
pluck it as
you sing. Plinky-
plonky. Rooty-toot.
Boy, that baby's
really cute!

PLAY IT AGAIN

Earth is an orchestra,
haven't you heard?
What are you waiting for?
Play me the world!

Play me the wind,
its whine and its whistle,
an egg as it cracks,
a sausage, its sizzle.

Play me the chatter
of children in class,
the plink of a pencil,
the chink of a glass.

A snap of a twig,
two wings in a flap.
Play me the drip
of a drop of a tap.

The rustle of paper,
the crash of a wave,
an echo (yes, echo),
from far in a cave.

If time is our rhythm,
then life is our song –
inviting us all
to go play along…

OUTSIDE/INDOORS

Where are you going?

Just popping outside.

Outside? What for?

To ride my bike.

Careful. It might be slippery.

Okay, will do.

And put your coat on. It's cold today.

Sure.

And a scarf. It looks freezing out there.

Fine.

And pop your gloves in your pockets, you never know.

Right.

Oh, and wear your new hat. It might just snow.

Yep... anything else?

Ah... don't forget your wellies, there may be huge puddles.

Mmm...

And don't go far, there could be a storm later.

A storm? A massive, evil storm that might blow me and my bike up into the sky, transport me a million miles away and then leave me stranded on a mountain top somewhere, freezing to death with only hungry bears to keep me company? Or even dropped into the vast ocean, only to be swallowed by the world's biggest ever whale – and I'll have to live the rest of my life trapped in its belly, surviving on a diet of raw fish and crabs – whilst I grow a beard longer than Rapunzel's hair? Or maybe hurled out into deep dark space where I'll orbit the earth on my bike forever and ever and ever and ev—

Oh don't be so silly! Hey – where are you off to now?

Nowhere. Can't be bothered. Think I'll stay indoors.

★ 45 ★

FIVE WAYS TO CROSS THE . . .

Build a rickety **R**aft with 10,000 lolly sticks

Cling to the w**I**ngs of a passing angel

Ride on the backs of fi**V**e black swans

Burrow a tunn**E**l way down below

Or see if there's a b**R**idge maybe...

THE POND

Now it seems
like a dream
that June afternoon
when we found
the pond
by the path.

And the pond
was alive, brimful,
bristling, wriggling
with brand new life.

And you cupped
your hands,
skimmed through
the water,
as one little tickler
twitched in your palm;
just a blob for a body
and a pointy tail,
so black, like soot,
like a miniature whale:
such a restless soul
is a tadpole.

SWEET MEADOW

The short cut
to the sweet shop
was a meadow wild
with summer flowers.

Those afternoons
were hazy-hot,
that high sun
burnt amber-bright,
and so we'd slowly
go the mile
to the shop.

Heading home
with paper bags,
we'd stop and swap
our blackjacks,
our white mice,
our multi-coloured
chocolate drops:
then sugar-fingered
sit amongst the grass
and scoff the lot.

That meadow
is a road now; cars
swiftly pass today,
the grass verges
neatly cut, a dandelion
clock remains:
half-blown away.

```
        @@@@                    @@@@
       @@@@@                   @@@@@
        @@@@                    @@@@
        ! ! !                   ! ! !
         ! !                     ! !
          !                       !
          !                       !
```

A hill if you will
is where time stands still
is where land kisses sky
is where kites learn to fly
is where clouds start to cry
where we walk you and I
to escape for a while
up the street now the stile
up a steep jagged mile
then we stop then we sit
at the top for a bit
and we chat this and that
looking down at the town
such a thrill it's brill is a hill

They wouldn't le**T** you near it now.

Too wild t**H**ey'd say. Yet

we were there, nearly **E**very day.

In that w**O**od, we were

the wild ones, free to **L**ive. Free to get lost.

And we **D**id.

We built a den. **W**e leapt over streams.

We sat in the chattering trees. **O**r made maps, or set traps

or fought the invading Vikings. **O**ne rule, hard and fast:

we had to be home by **D**ark.

WILD!

Wild the garden overgrown
wild the jaw that breaks the bone

Wild the rain that soaks the sand
wild the sun that cracks the land

Wild the summer's green and greed
wild the wind that sows the seed

Wild the flower, big in bloom
wild the early dawning tune

Wild the bird that seeks the sun
wild the cry when life is done

Wild the claw that rips the skin
wild the bite, the tear, the sting

Wild the young that feed to grow
wild the blood that stains the snow

Wild the stench of fresh decay
wild the mulch that rots away

Wild the winter's yearly cull
wild the springtime's early bulb

Wild the thorn, the fruit, the bud
wild the roots, the shoots, the mud

Wild the song, the forest hum
wild the rhythm in the drum

Wild the honey in the comb
wild the hunter heading home

Wild the worm that breaks the soil
wild the world in constant toil

Wild the weed that lives in cracks
wild the scythe, the saw, the axe

Wild the heart at trees laid bare
wild that wild no longer there

BETWEEN THE DOG AND THE WOLF

(after Aesop)

A wolf once chanced upon a dog
outside the wild wood.
Cried Wolf, 'And how are you today?'
Barked Dog, 'Well, life is good:

I'm loved, I'm fed, and warm's my bed.
So me, I'm doing fine!'
'Fed?' cried Wolf, and 'Warm?' he said.
'I'd swap your life for mine.'

'I'm starved,' moaned Wolf, 'I'm cold. Afraid.
My life is constant strain.
And every day I struggle on
through wind, through snow, through rain.'

'But what,' asked Wolf, 'is that odd thing?'
'Oh that!' laughed Dog, 'it's great! –
My collar's how they tie me up
so I will not escape!

And that's not all, it bears my name!
I run when I am called!
Or fetch a stick, or do a trick.
A dog is not ignored!'

'A name?' cried Wolf, 'Have you no shame?
A beast must keep its soul.
You're better dead than tame.' he said.
'You have been truly sold…

However hard my life may get
my spirit must be free.
I'll keep my moon, my stars, my dark,
my space to live and be.'

With this, the Wolf began to cry
a tortured, whining growl –
so horrified by brother Dog:
that's how it learnt to howl.

★ 55 ★

SPOT THE FREAKY FABLE

(HAIKU)

(after Aesop)

Outcome curious:
tortoise was victorious.
Hare was furious!

BROWN OWL

How
now, brown
owl! ◉ What's ◉ with
the scowl? And why the ruffle
of your windswept wings? And
those glaring eyes, like two gold
rings! Are your neighbours loud?
Is the moon too bright? Is there
something on your mind tonight? Hey, don't fly off,
you come back now,
and tell me your
secrets, old
brown owl!
mm   mm
mmm   mmm

>>

CROW

Come Crow, bring down the night.
Spread wide those scraggy, wizened wings.
Swoop low. Dive deep. Take flight.

With sharpened beak, peck out the stars,
each one by one from charcoal sky.
And from that mind of soot and scars

work your crafty charms of old
and send whole cities off to sleep
then leave us blind and cold.

Drum up shadows, dusty ghosts,
and those that dwell in dark.
Free their ancient, broken souls.

Swap moon for sun then go.
The day is dead. Your work is done.
The night has come, old Crow.

WHAT THE MOUSE SAID

Listen.

If you really think there's a silent night
then you don't know what the dark is like.

Please trust me, folks. I've been around –
the night's a symphony of sound.

The slightest breath vibrates my whiskers.
Hear how snow falls hushed like whispers?

Hey, what's that? A tummy's rumble?
Baby's snuffle? Old man's mumble?

There. A fox invades a garden,
knocks a bin, then scarpers barking.

Oh, the breeze, its twisted song:
the trees can't help but jig along.

Folks, you don't know what you're missing –
stay awake tonight and *listen…*

SO YOU WANT TO BUILD A BEAR...

A bear must see.
For eyes, find orbs,
winter-brown and wet
with all the sorrows
of the world.

A bear must wonder.
Fill its head with questions,
a curiosity for all things:
anthills, beehives, even
the movements of the moon.

Add to this another hunger,
from having dreamt
the dark days through.

A bear must fish.
Take a coat of rich fur
to keep out the river's chill;
give it paws crowned
with five fine claws.

A bear must eat.
Set teeth as tough as bullets
into two wide jaws.

Cut its shadow
from the silence
of the ancient earth.

A bear must roam.
Give it limbs, strong
and tall, to wander through
the forest. Spring, summer, fall.

Don't forget the snout.
A bear must sniff out where it is
and has to go: up the trail,
off the track, to a cave snug and deep.
That's enough. Come away.
A bear must sleep.

SLEEP

Sleep is a city
of towers and walls
a forest of whispers and
charming young wolves

Sleep is a castle
of shadows and mist
a century burst by
a spell-breaking kiss

Sleep is a dreamer
as well as a guide
through gardens and mazes
and maps of your mind

Sleep is a potion
not poison, but kind
to help you escape
leave night-time behind

Sleep is a cloud
adrift on the land
a trickle like silver
that slips through your hand

Sleep is a nest
and a rest deep and lush
a heartful of wonder
a headful of hush

SUNRISE-SUNWISE

Wake up, all you
sleepy peeps – you **earth-lings** need to know... that I'm a
star, I really am, **sol**-ebrity magnifico.
Your sun?!? I'm **Mum**, that's **cosmically** – for
you were truly made by me (in **Big Bang** time,
pre-history). And though I'm old, my hair's still
gold, and outer **space** may be so cold but I'm
so cool, cos I'm so **hot** and have been since
the year **dot**. There's plenty fire left in me –
five more **billion** years – you'll see. No,
I'm not one for modesty – I'm
literally quite *BRILLIANT*,
me !!!!!!!

BONUS BITS

ABOUT THE AUTHOR

An award-winning children's poet, James Carter travels all over the cosmos (well, Britain) with his guitar (that's Keith) to give lively poetry performances and workshops. A regular visitor to festivals and libraries, James has been to over 1200 Primary schools in the last 14 years. Phew!

jamescarterpoet.co.uk

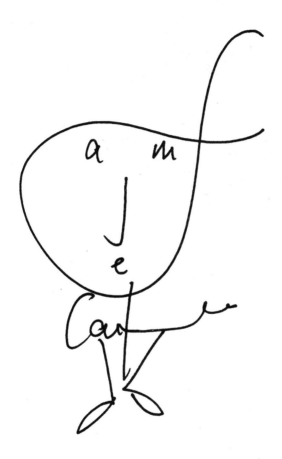

DREAM ON...

or... James answers some popular questions

HAVE YOU ALWAYS BEEN A POET?

Maybe! I've always been a space cadet you see –
a dreamer – and for me, poems are the best place to
put all my daydreamy thoughts. A poem takes
months of dreaming and writing. For this book,
I wrote hundreds of poems, but only 46 got in.
That's a lot of dreaming...

WHY DO YOU WRITE AND PLAY GUITAR?

Because! I've been playing the guitar since I was 15,
so that's... ouch – 42 years! As a teenager, I had really
long hair (honestly) and I was in a very noisy, nasty
rock band. We did a vinyl single produced by the
singer from Deep Purple. I still play and write
guitar pieces. All my guitars are called 'Keith'.

'Keith'?!?

I've also got a melodica – a mini piano – called 'Steve'.

'Steve'?!?

Why not?

WHERE DO YOU GET YOUR IDEAS FROM?

Weird question – EVERYTHING is an idea! I'm not
a fiction writer, so I don't need to invent anything –
I'm simply inspired to write about the things in my
life or the world around me, or even the world at large.
The cat from two doors down bullied our kittens,
so I wrote 'Sid' (p6). We walked up my favourite hill
in Streatley one Fathers' Day, so I wrote the hill poem
(p50). We met a pretend moonwalker, so I wrote about
that too (p33).

As a poet, it's not so much 'WHERE' you get your
ideas from, but 'WHAT' you choose to write about,
and then 'HOW' do you write about it – for instance,
should it be a shape poem or kenning or haiku?
Should I write the words ǝpᴉsdn uʍop or in a
WEIRD FONT or in massive

CAPITAL
LETTERS?

Poets are, in the main, non-fiction writers, and my job is
to find new or creative ways of writing about things – I
want to say 'Hey, look at THAT... but look at it like THIS!'

WHAT ADVICE DO YOU HAVE?

Simple: read, read, write, write. The more you read and write, the better your writing will be. Try writing different things – poems, stories, comic strips, your autobiography, a non-fiction booklet, a short play. If you have a thought or if something happens in your life, write about it. Draw and doodle too. And do your writing just for you. You don't even need to show it to anyone.

DO YOU LIKE BEING A POET?

No! I love it. I love words – I'm a 'word-nerd'. I love writing books, and I love all the other things I do – travelling all over the country, acting a bit daft, reading my poems, playing Keith/Steve wherever I go, and above all, encouraging others to write too. What's not to like?

WHAT'S YOUR FAVOURITE...?

Colour? Blue. *Number?* Seven. *Children's film?* WALL.E. *Children's book?* Where The Wild Things Are. *Animal?* Wolf. *Music?* The Beatles. *Food?* Porridge.

HOW WOULD CHANGE SCHOOLS IF YOU COULD?

There would be 10 minutes of daydreaming in every school every single day...